Healing after Loss

Rebound from Hardship and Heartache

GREGORY L. JANTZ, PHD
WITH KEITH WALL

AspirePress

Healing After Loss:
Rebound from Hardship and Heartache

Published by Aspire Press,
an imprint of Tyndale House Ministries,
Carol Stream, Illinois
rose-publishing.com

ISBN: 978-1-4964-8131-3

The views and opinions expressed in this book are those of the author(s) and do not necessarily express the views of Tyndale House Ministries or Aspire Press, nor is this book intended to be a substitute for mental health treatment or professional counseling. The information in this resource is intended as a guideline for healthy living. Please consult qualified medical, legal, pastoral, and psychological professionals regarding individual concerns.

Tyndale House Ministries and Aspire Press are in no way liable for any content, change of content, or activity for the works listed. Citation of a work does not mean endorsement of all its contents or of other works by the same author.

Printed in the United States of America
31 30 29 28 27 26 25
7 6 5 4 3 2 1

Contents

FOREWORD

Dear Reader:

It's just like God to arrange for the book you have in your hand to be a gift to me as well. As a reminder to both of us here at the outset, I've included the Scripture verse cited on one of its last pages:

> I focus on this one thing: Forgetting the past and looking forward to what lies ahead, I press on to reach the end of the race and receive the heavenly prize for which God, through Christ Jesus, is calling us. (Philippians 3:13–14 NLT)

You see, I, too, have experienced a loss. As this book prepares to go to press, my family and I are mourning the fresh loss of Dr. Jantz. He was my husband and my hiking buddy. He was father and mentor to my two sons. And his death is still very fresh in our minds.

While his homegoing is a marvelous truth, we who are left behind grieve. As I write this, it still seems surreal that my husband—my life partner and best friend—has left this world for an eternity with Jesus, the One he loved and served. It is because of Jesus that Gregg wanted to understand and care for those affected by the abuse, trauma, and hurt of this fallen world.

The book you are reading now was written by Gregg with the desire to provide hope to those facing their darkest hour, when all hope seems lost. I can't imagine he had our family in mind when these pages were typed, and yet his entire work has been based around giving hope to those who are traumatized, to those facing addiction, and yes—even to those who have become widows and orphans.

When he started his work in the field of whole-person care, Gregg sought to bring hope to the hurting. *The Center: A Place of Hope*, located on the beautiful Puget Sound in Edmonds, Washington, continues to do this day in and day out, as individuals who arrive there are met with caring staff and a hope-filled plan.

My prayer for you is that this book will offer some comfort as it helps you move toward healing, providing a sweet and gentle reminder that God is always with you through his precious Son, Jesus. Hold on to the hope found in Philippians 3!

LaFon Jantz
Edmonds, WA, July 2025

INTRODUCTION

When Loss Invades Your Life

Chances are that you picked up this book because you are struggling with the pain of loss and grief that has invaded your life. You are seeking comfort and healing at a time when your heart aches and you feel doubtful that you can become whole again. You might wonder if you can ever regain the joy and inner peace you experienced before your loss.

There's a good chance, too, that you are courageous and tenacious, because you are choosing to take the first steps—or further steps—on your path toward wholeness and well-being.

Every person on earth experiences loss at some time in their life. From some losses you may be able to recover relatively quickly, but others reshape your life and leave pain and grief in their wake for a long time to come. Since

I work as a psychologist, I frequently hear the details of my clients' struggles with grief. They tell me things like ...

- "Ever since I lost my spouse, I have felt so depressed that I can hardly get out of bed in the morning."
- "My marriage of twenty years ended in divorce, and now I feel lost and aimless."
- "After I broke my back in a car accident and lost mobility, I started taking painkillers, and now they've taken over my life."
- "When my son died, I felt like I died too. In fact, a big part of me really did die."

Statements like these are made by people who feel mired in the pain of their loss with little hope for brighter days ahead. But there is hope for healing—hope that is rooted in inner strength, abundant resilience, support from others, and our all-powerful Creator. My responses to my clients' pleas of desperation usually go like this:

- "It *is* possible get over this time of hurt and heartache. I believe you can and you will."
- "Your pain is real and deep, but it doesn't have to hold you captive. It doesn't have to determine who you are."

- "Life brings us plenty of challenges, but as you persevere and overcome, the future can still hold joyful adventures for you."

I say these same things to you as you seek to work through the strong emotions that accompany your painful loss. You *can* be free from thoughts and feelings that pull you down rather than lift you up.

EVERY PERSON ON EARTH EXPERIENCES LOSS AT SOME TIME IN THEIR LIFE.

But I am not giving you a pep talk or offering snappy slogans to help you feel better momentarily. The last thing you need is advice that rings hollow or promises that deliver little. If you've been struggling with painful loss, you've likely heard all kinds of recommendations that haven't brought much improvement. Worse, you've probably heard plenty of clichés from well-meaning (but unhelpful) people—sentiments such as "Just let it go," or "This too shall pass," or "Hold on to your faith."

Rest assured, I know that working through loss is not easy. It takes patience, fierce determination, courage to confront painful issues, openness to new ideas, and a commitment to adapt to new life circumstances.

The American Psychological Association (APA) describes *resilience* as "the process of adapting well in the face of adversity, trauma, tragedy, threats, or significant sources of stress."[1] One could also say that resilience is the ability to get back up when you've been knocked down by the roughness of life.

The APA also says that "while certain factors might make some individuals more resilient than others, resilience isn't necessarily a personality trait that only some people possess. On the contrary, resilience involves behaviors, thoughts, and actions that anyone can learn and develop."

As a devout person of faith, I firmly believe that God wants the very best for all who follow him. Over and over, Scripture confirms that God desires for us to live with joy, fulfillment, and peace. Naturally, and sadly, we will not experience the fullness life has to offer when we struggle through unaddressed grief. But we can choose a much more hopeful and healing path forward by asking God for the insight, courage, and resilience we need to prevail over our circumstances.

Are you ready to start the journey of healing after loss—of rebounding from hardship and heartache? Let's begin by looking at how loss affects four important areas of your life.

CHAPTER 1

The Legacy of Loss

Anyone who has not yet experienced a traumatic loss might presume that its chief consequence is emotional distress, since loss can cause shock, disbelief, hurt, anguish, sadness, and anger. Truly, emotional turmoil is an oppressive, unwanted visitor following loss. But it doesn't take long to realize that loss brings hardship to *every* aspect of a person's life.

Finding your way back from heartache requires that you care for your whole self. As you begin to rebound from the distress and disorientation you're feeling, it will be helpful to understand how loss affects you not only emotionally but also in other key areas of your life, including your spirituality, relationships, and physical health.

1. Emotional Distress

There's no way around it: Loss hurts, and it can even reshape your life. Losing a loved one to death, divorce, or a breakup is emotionally devastating. Even after losing a job or a business—or your home to fire, flood, or storm—the heartbreak can be overwhelming. It would take an extremely calloused person to *not* experience emotional turmoil. Amid your painful and surreal loss, are you feeling …

- *Shocked?* Normal.
- *Sad?* Who wouldn't be?
- *Hurt, angry?* Perfectly understandable.

Yes, significant loss is tumultuous, so please understand this: It's okay to cry. It's okay to grieve. It's okay to not be okay for a while. As a caring human being, you're processing your loss with the emotional capacity your Creator gave you. Let your emotions do their work.

2. Relationship Strain

Veronica and Mateo's daughter had reached the age that their son, Manuel, had been when he died in a horrible accident. The situation they described is one I have witnessed many times in the aftermath of loss.

Veronica observed, "I've noticed that Mateo and I relate to our daughter differently. I've become more remote from Isabella and less involved, because I'm guarding my emotions and holding my fear at bay. I can't stand the thought that we could lose another child."

Mateo nodded his head in agreement while Veronica continued.

"As for Mateo, he's become overprotective—a helicopter parent. He hardly lets Isabella out of his sight and is always talking to her about safety, to the point where she sees the world as a dangerous and threatening place. It's understandable why he views life that way, but I think it's unhealthy to fill a little girl's head with dread and worry."

In the wake of significant loss, our supportive relationships often undergo a shift in dynamics, including conflict and codependency. Withdrawal from friends, a spouse, or other family members can also occur—because it's just too difficult to share painful thoughts and feelings with another person.

If your loss is recent and raw, some isolation and withdrawal might be helpful as you work through your feelings before trying to express them. But if isolation and withdrawal become the norm, your relationships may grow more distant and superficial.

3. Physical Symptoms

Your body has an intricate connection with your soul and emotions. When one dimension suffers, the others do as well. Many people are surprised to discover that after experiencing significant loss, their grief can actually trigger debilitating physical illness or pain.

In the turbulence of your loss, a variety of hormones and neurochemicals can flood your brain. Cortisol (sometimes called the "stress hormone") is often released more frequently and in higher quantities during grief. These elevated cortisol levels can impact your overall health, potentially resulting in high blood pressure or increased risk of heart disease.

While trying to process disbelief and sadness, it's also not uncommon to lack energy and sleep poorly. If this describes your experience, the result is that you're not just tired—you're weary. You are probably not eating well, either opting for unhealthy comfort foods or losing your appetite altogether. And exercise? Forget it. In the surreal state you're in, it's the last thing you want to do.

IN THE WAKE OF LOSS, OUR RELATIONSHIPS OFTEN UNDERGO A SHIFT IN DYNAMICS.

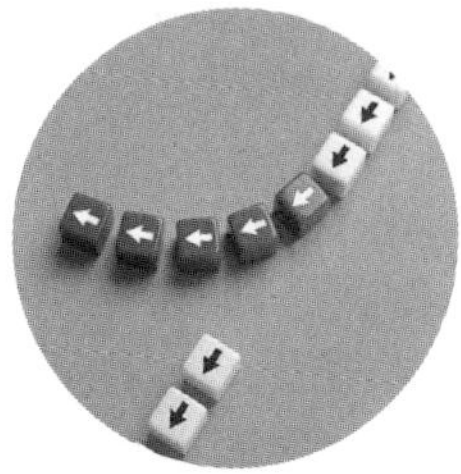

4. Spiritual Confusion

Does your loss leave you feeling abandoned or betrayed by God? This is a common aftereffect for those who have endured heartache of any kind. I can't tell you how many times people have expressed their spiritual confusion in the wake of loss. Here are a few examples:

- "My daughter lost her battle with cancer sixteen years ago, and I still feel the pain all these years later. We were a devout family that served God. Where was he?"

- "My parents split after twenty years of marriage. I prayed and prayed that their relationship would be restored, but it didn't happen."

Without a doubt, the significant losses of life can profoundly affect our spiritual beliefs in different ways. Some draw closer to God's comforting presence, while others don't want anything to do with him. Some shake their fists at God, accusing him of not caring and failing to protect.

WHILE PROCESSING LOSS, IT'S NOT UNCOMMON TO LACK ENERGY AND SLEEP POORLY.

Be assured that God can handle your full range of emotions. He has compassion for you as you grieve, question, complain, and even rage at him. If you no longer feel God's presence or believe that he has abandoned you, it does not change the fact that he is grieving with you and loves you deeply. God has promised his children, "Never will I leave you; never will I forsake you" (Hebrews 13:5). We must choose whether to make our relationship with him deeper with trust or more distant with doubt.

How Will You Respond?

The whole-person treatment approach recognizes that every human being is a unique constellation of emotional, relational, physical, and spiritual dimensions. Your loss has cut so deeply into each of these areas because you loved and cared so deeply.

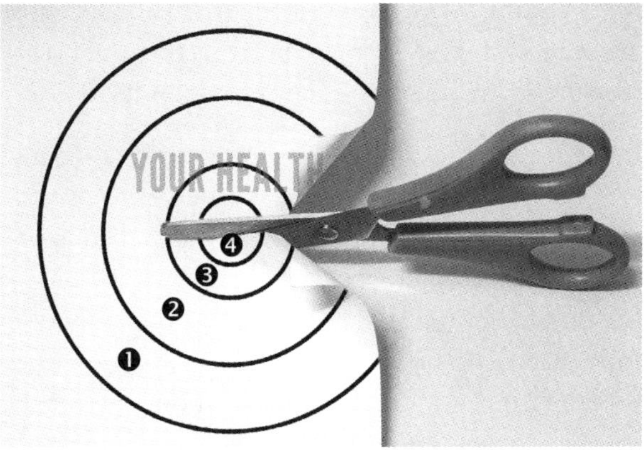

❶ Emotional ❷ Relational ❸ Physical ❹ Spiritual

Recovery will take time. It will also take prayer, faith, self-discipline, and the courage to engage in the fullness of life again. As you embark on your journey, consider the following suggestions.

1 Be Willing to Hope

I have counseled thousands of people who needed help coping with pain and fear of every kind: grief, anxiety, depression, anger, addiction, and the emotional scars of physical and psychological abuse. Early in my career, I often felt dismayed by the epic scope of battles people waged within themselves and their elusive struggle to achieve true healing. It seemed that lasting wellness was a treasure many sought but few ever found.

Then I realized something vitally important: Many of the hurting people I counseled were eager to overcome their troubles, but they lacked the key ingredient of *hope*. Distress and despair, caused by significant loss, were compounded by a fundamental lack of hopefulness and confidence that anything would ever change. Hurting people often do not feel enthused about the future, if they can envision one at all.

This led me to make *hope* a cornerstone of my counseling practice, speaking engagements, and writing projects. My team and I also adopted Jeremiah 29:11–12 as our clinic's guiding Scripture passage:

> "I know the plans I have for you," declares the Lord, "plans to prosper you and not to harm you, plans to give you hope and a future. Then you will

> call on me and come and pray to me, and I will listen to you. You will seek me and find me when you seek me with all your heart. I will be found by you," declares the LORD, "and will bring you back from captivity."

I encourage you to reflect on these life-changing words and embrace them as your touchstone as you pursue your own emotional, relational, physical, and spiritual wellness. After all, dealing with loss can often make you feel that you are in a "captivity" of sorts—trapped and immobilized by a force bigger than yourself. But if you hold on to the smallest seed of hope, it will, over time, blossom into comfort and strength.

God can help you rebound from hardship and heartache as well as renew your dreams and refresh your energy to achieve them. His Word promises that "those who hope in the LORD will renew their strength. They will soar on wings like eagles; they will run and not grow weary, they will walk and not be faint" (Isaiah 40:31).

2 Be Willing to Listen

As the adage goes, the first step to fixing a problem is admitting you have one. But many times we have blind spots, especially when we're grieving a loss. Is it possible that someone you trust—a family member, friend, counselor, or colleague—has noticed you've developed harmful behaviors or habits in the wake of your loss? If so, do you tend to get angry or defensive when they mention their observation?

> "THOSE WHO HOPE IN THE LORD WILL RENEW THEIR STRENGTH."
>
> –Isaiah 40:31

Often, we are already aware of the negative habits or behaviors that we're struggling with, but we feel overwhelmed or exhausted at the thought of addressing them. Or perhaps we succumb to denial and refuse to look squarely at the harmful actions and attitudes we've adopted after our painful experiences. But in order to move in a positive life direction, it's essential that we acknowledge our own observations and those of others.

3 Be Willing to Heal

It's okay if you don't know where to begin or even exactly what issues are causing problems. I often hear my clients say something like, "I don't really know why I'm here. I just know that something is not right, and I want to figure out what's going on." Another common remark I hear is, "My spouse says that I need therapy, but I think I'm doing just fine."

The person who is willing to seek help—even if they're not sure what exactly is wrong—is a lot closer to finding healing than the person who is not. To face loss is to take a courageous, giant step toward healing. Here are a few reasons why:

- Addressing your loss is the only way through it.
- You will have greater peace and joy.
- You will regain a sense of power and control in your life.
- You will be equipped to help others deal with their own grief.

In the next chapter, we'll take a look at how the grieving process is a vital first step as you progress toward healing.

STEPPING STONES TO HEALING

1. **Pay attention to your emotional health.** Engage with a helpful book or podcast that addresses your emotional needs in the wake of loss, or make the bold move to seek professional counseling.

   Takeaways: ____

   ____

   ____

   ____

   ____

2. **Transform a difficult relationship.** Perhaps your loss has changed the dynamics of your relationships. Identify one action you can take to build bridges, such as expressing your desire for reconciliation or planning a shared activity that you both enjoy.

   My action: ____

   ____

3. **Bolster your physical health.** Choose one of the following options; then slowly build from there:

   - Start (or restart) an exercise routine for twenty minutes, three times a week. This can be as simple as taking a walk in your neighborhood.

- Include more nutritious foods in your diet while reducing sugary and processed comfort foods.
- Start a nightly sleep routine to ensure proper rest.

My option: ______________________________

____

4. **Nurture your spiritual life.** Set aside time to seek God and rest in his presence:
   - Read a psalm from the Bible or a passage from a devotional book, or search online for free devotional resources.
   - Spend a few minutes seeking God in prayer.
   - Listen to inspiring worship music or encouraging teachings from a trusted minister.

Takeaways: ______________________________

____

____

____

____

CHAPTER 2

A Time to Grieve

On the hot, humid afternoon of July 4, 1939, nearly sixty-two thousand spectators crammed into Yankee Stadium, but a strange hush soon descended over the normally boisterous crowd at "The House That Ruth Built." Although Babe Ruth was in attendance, the fans had not come to see their famous Hall of Fame slugger, now in his fourth year of retirement. They had gathered to pay tribute to Lou Gehrig.

Playing alongside Ruth for a dozen seasons, Gehrig helped the New York Yankees achieve remarkable success, winning seven World Series championships in his career. Individually, Gehrig earned seven straight All-Star Game appearances, two American League MVP awards, and one Triple Crown. Dubbed "The Iron Horse," Gehrig was as durable as he was talented. Starting on June 1, 1925, Gehrig played in a remarkable

2,130 consecutive games, a record that stood for fifty-six years, until Cal Ripken Jr. broke the mark in 1995. On April 30, 1939, Gehrig voluntarily ended his own streak when he removed himself from the lineup after he didn't play well. By then, it was clear that a mysterious ailment was impeding his performance. Soon thereafter, Gehrig visited Mayo Clinic in Rochester, Minnesota, where he received a harrowing diagnosis: amyotrophic lateral sclerosis, or ALS, which came to be known as "Lou Gehrig's Disease."

ALS is a degenerative disease that affects nerve cells in the brain and spinal cord, resulting in weakened muscles, difficult swallowing, and impaired speech. Eventually, those with ALS lose control of the muscles needed for life-sustaining functions, including eating and breathing. Gehrig's diagnosis was a virtual death sentence, with no known cure to this day.

Before the disease started affecting his on-field performance in 1938, Gehrig was in the prime of his career. Off the field, he was happily married to his wife, Eleanor, and had even enjoyed a starring role (playing himself) in the 1938 movie *Rawhide*. But by 1939, he was so weak that during his "Lou Gehrig Appreciation Day" ceremony at Yankee Stadium, he needed to set down each of his gifts after he received them.

Yet as Gehrig addressed the crowd from a microphone at home plate, self-pity was nowhere to be found. "For the past two weeks," he said, "you have been reading about a bad break. Yet today I consider myself the luckiest man on the face of the earth."[2] Less than two years later—on June 2, 1941—Gehrig died. He was only thirty-seven.

Loss Is Inevitable

Thankfully, most of us won't experience anything like what Lou Gehrig suffered. But every human being will experience loss of some kind. It's important to know that in your struggle with loss and grief, you are not alone. In fact, one study found that nearly 72 percent of respondents had grieved a life event over the previous three-year period, including:[3]

- **32%** Death of a parent, sibling, extended-family member, or close friend
- **29%** Loss of a friendship or close relationship
- **23%** Diagnosis of a loved one's serious illness or chronic health condition
- **20%** Death of a pet

15% Diagnosis of their own serious illness or chronic health condition

11% Loss of a job

4% Divorce

4% Loss of a home or possessions

3% Death of a spouse

2% Death of a child

How we deal with loss makes all the difference in the world. Will we try to avoid the bad news as long as possible? Will we try to pretend everything is okay in a relationship, even when the evidence—and all our friends—tell us otherwise? Over the course of my counseling career, I've noticed that a few common traits characterize those who avoid acknowledging and grieving their losses:

- They try to suppress their heartache but aren't usually successful.
- They are easily angered.

- Their loss negatively affects their attitude and perspective, robbing them of rich life experiences.
- They sometimes choose to soothe their heartache by making harmful choices that can lead to addiction.

The trauma of loss likes to hide in the dark recesses of our hearts, away from the light of day. The sad fact is that many people don't achieve healing after loss because they never examine and address the source of their pain. After all, why go back and revisit the painful moments of life? We're wired to avoid pain, yet grieving a loss is necessary for true healing to take place.

GRIEVING A LOSS IS NECESSARY FOR TRUE HEALING TO TAKE PLACE.

What Is Grief?

Grief is a word we're all too familiar with, and one that we would rather mention in the context of others' pain instead of our own. We associate grief with feelings and behaviors that range from sadness to weeping to emotional numbness to depression. You might also relate to the detailed definition provided by the American Psychological Association (APA):

> Grief is the anguish experienced after significant loss, usually the death of a beloved person.
>
> Grief often includes physiological distress, separation anxiety, confusion, yearning, obsessive dwelling on the past, and apprehension about the future. Intense grief can become life-threatening through disruption of the immune system, self-neglect, and suicidal thoughts.
>
> Grief may also take the form of regret for something lost, remorse for something done, or sorrow for a mishap to oneself.[4]

As this definition suggests, grief is most often associated with the death of someone close to us—a parent, spouse, child, sibling, or friend. But grief is also caused by countless other losses, including:

- The end of a marriage or long-term romantic relationship
- The death of a beloved pet
- A business going bankrupt
- The destruction of a cherished home in a disaster
- Physical or mental abilities due to accident, illness, or injury

- The end or straining of a close friendship or family relationship because of conflict, relocation, or other difficult circumstances

In short, grief is caused by *any* loss that generates feelings of deep sadness, remorse, emptiness, longing, and anguish. I could go on and on listing the losses we might endure, so feel free to add your own experience to the list.

It is all too evident that painful loss and the grief that follows are unfortunate facts of life. A wise step toward healing is to ask, *How does the grieving process work?* To help lay the foundation for your journey, let's explore how three important characteristics of grief and the five stages of grief affect your recovery.

Three Characteristics *of* Grief

1 Grief Is Personal and Deeply Felt

Recently I spoke with an eighty-one-year-old woman whose fourteen-year-old dachshund had passed away. A widow for twenty years, her beloved dog had been her constant companion and comfort for a significant portion of that time. Describing her grief, this woman used the word *traumatizing*, and no doubt that's exactly what the experience was for her.

Other people might consider the loss of a pet to be sad but not devastating. Likewise, some people might regard a job loss as a mere setback, while others would experience it as a traumatic event. The point is that no one should decide for anyone else what is or is not a painful loss or cause for grief.

2 Everyone's Grief Journey Is Different

Phrases such as "Time heals all wounds" and "Just give it time" may represent some of the most misleading, unhelpful advice we can receive following a traumatic loss. It is true that some people have reserves of resilience that allow them to bounce back after a period of recovery, but this is far better explained by the fact that we all respond differently to grief. There is not a timeframe that applies to all people. There is no specific stage you should be at for any given amount of time. There is no end date.

Different activities and practices will bring different levels of comfort to each individual. Everyone is unique in how they experience their emotions in the present moment, how they choose to cope with their pain, and how they grieve as time passes.

In the coping phase, friends and family can be incredibly helpful—or incredibly unhelpful. Lots of people have advice for how you should react and respond to your loss, but you should sift through this advice selectively, picking out the wise gems and tossing the rest. You can give yourself the freedom to pursue healing in the way and at the pace that you deem best for yourself.

3 Healing Takes More than Willpower

Some people mistakenly believe that sorrow and anguish will go away if they keep pressing on. It's true that willpower, determination, and grit are helpful in allowing you to take steps forward. But they are not enough to achieve lasting peace and wellness, since grief deeply impacts most every area of your life—emotionally, physically, relationally, and spiritually.

When grief is overwhelming and powerful, it can seem to have no end. Grief this extensive is called *complicated grief,* which affects between 10 to 20 percent of those who are dealing with loss.[5] Emotions become overwhelming, and daily functioning is difficult. Since this can go on for a long time, those experiencing complicated grief will need additional support and guidance to process their loss.

The Five Stages of Grief

When it comes to understanding grief and how to move through the process, Elisabeth Kübler-Ross's well-known Five Stages of Grief is a helpful tool. It should be noted that grief does not necessarily follow these stages in sequential order. In fact, the process of healing often finds a person moving back and forth through these stages at various times. Still, this model provides valuable insight into what most grieving people experience in some way, to some degree.[6] Let's discuss how each stage relates to healing after loss.

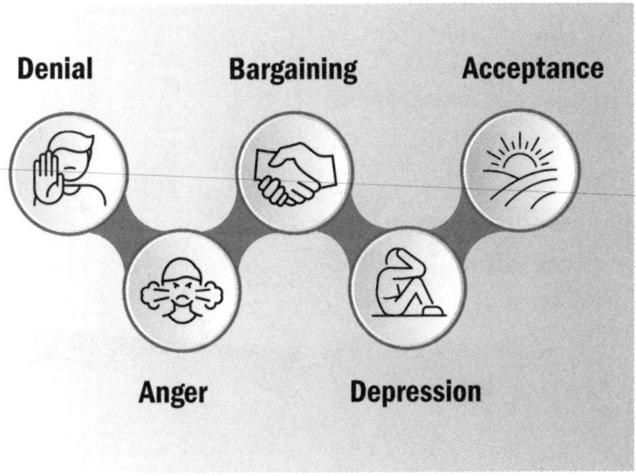

1. Denial

When you suffer a significant loss, your survival instincts take over as you shift into fight-or-flight mode. Your brain will do whatever it takes to protect you from life-threatening dangers, so your first response might be to protect yourself by denying the event. That's why people dealing with significant loss often struggle with thoughts such as:

- *I can't believe my brother died … This can't be happening!*
- *Divorce happens to other people, but not to me …*
- *There's no way my career is ending because of this injury!*

The length of the denial stage usually corresponds to the intensity of the loss. For example, if you barely knew your recently deceased Uncle Charlie, the denial stage may be short or nonexistent. On the other hand, it will be more difficult to accept and grieve the absence of someone you knew and loved well.

2. Anger

This stage often stems from a feeling of abandonment following loss. Many people become stuck in the anger stage. Getting past anger can be quite difficult, especially when you have been abandoned, abused, or otherwise wronged. In such cases, please be assured that forgiving the person who contributed to your loss does not excuse their behavior. Rather, working through your anger to the point of forgiveness frees *you* from bearing the pain and loss associated with their actions.

GOD INVITES YOU TO BE HONEST WITH HIM ABOUT YOUR ANGER AND BITTERNESS.

Some people also experience anger toward God for allowing their loss, while others realize that God in his loving mercy can help ease their burden of anger and bitterness. Second Corinthians 1:3–4 says, "Praise be to the God and Father of our Lord Jesus Christ, the Father of compassion and the God of all comfort, who comforts us in all our troubles." God invites you to be honest with him about your anger and bitterness.

The ability to process anger takes courage and wisdom. This is not to be taken lightly, and you will probably need plenty of help from others to move forward. Take however much time you need.

3. Bargaining

This stage of grief may be marked by persistent thoughts about what could have been done to prevent or somehow reverse the loss. Bargaining is a common trait, especially among children, who are not yet able to process loss effectively. Whether it's the divorce of their parents, the death of a loved one, or another traumatic loss, they may believe they did something to cause it or that they could have somehow prevented it. When these false beliefs are not corrected, they often persist into adulthood. I know many adults who have carried decades-old shame and guilt over losses that were not their fault.

4. Depression

Perhaps the most difficult part of the grief process, depression can set in when you begin to realize the full weight of your loss. In many cases, facing those sad or emotionally intense feelings leads to depressive behavior as you experience negative changes in your thoughts and actions. Emotional upheaval from a traumatic loss—such as a severe or chronic illness, a significant disappointment with a job or family, or the illness or death of a loved one—destabilizes your ability to cope, making you even more susceptible to falling into depression.

As with the anger stage, it's very important to lean on your friends and loved ones for help, as well as a professional counselor or therapist. Allow your safe circle to know that you need their support as you process several complex emotions during your grief journey. I love the proverb that says, "Victory is won through many advisers" (Proverbs 24:6). You can wage war against depression with wise, trusted counsel.

5. Acceptance

When you reach the acceptance stage, you can say, "The loss I experienced was painful and hard. However, it no longer has a grip on me. As I process my grief in healthy ways and let go of my anger, hurt, and bitterness, I am taking steps toward freedom."

Our recovery journey after loss is often like hiking switchbacks on a mountain trail. As we double back, it may seem like we're not making progress when we look down and see the trail that we just walked on. But we must remember that with each step we take along the way, we are still climbing the mountain. Keep going! You'll reach the summit.

From Grief *to* Growth

I began this chapter with the story about Lou Gehrig's loss of health and athletic prowess. But his journey didn't end there. Gehrig could have responded in a number of negative ways: He could have lived in denial, grown bitter, or even given up. But he didn't.

Gehrig continued to travel with the Yankees as a nonplaying captain for the remainder of the 1939 season. And just a few months after his "luckiest man" speech, he accepted an offer from Mayor Fiorello La Guardia to become a New York City parole commissioner, after turning down more lucrative speaking and appearance offers. With the help of his wife, Gehrig visited his parole commission office often, as well as various correctional facilities. He continued to serve in that role until a month before his death in June 1941, when he was barely able to walk.

Gehrig's example of grace, dignity, and strength amid his tremendous loss left a lifetime impression on many people. He courageously acknowledged his severe trial for what it was and continued to make the world a better place in the time he had left. With God's comfort and the help of trusted advisers, you, too, can meet the hardship of loss and grief head-on, with grace, dignity, and strength.

As Solomon, the writer of the book of Ecclesiastes, proclaimed, there is "a time to mourn" (3:4), but there is also "a time to heal" (3:3). In the next chapter, we will explore several steps you can take to progress on your journey of healing after loss.

STEPPING STONES TO HEALING

1. **Explore the Five Stages of Grief.** Does a particular stage resonate with you at the moment? Have you noticed yourself moving back and forth between certain stages? Remember that healing after loss takes time, patience, and gentleness.

   Takeaways: ______________________________

   ____

   ____

   ____

   ____

   ____

   ____

2. **Open up to trusted loved ones.** Remember the proverb I mentioned? There is wisdom and strength in wise counsel. Share your grief with a close friend or family member and let them help shoulder your load.

   Takeaways: ______________________________

   ____

   ____

   ____

   ____

   ____

   ____

3. **Seek professional help if needed.** The grieving process is difficult to navigate—but vital for healing. If the process is overwhelming you beyond the support available to you through friends and family, consider finding a reputable and caring therapist, counselor, or support group.

   Takeaways: ________________________________

   ____

   ____

   ____

   ____

   ____

   ____

4. **Don't hold yourself back from weeping.** As you work through the grief process, tears most likely will come. That's good! Let them flow. Tears are not a sign of weakness. Rather, they reveal deep emotions and show that you are courageously confronting hard issues.

   Takeaways: ________________________________

   ____

   ____

   ____

   ____

   ____

   ____

CHAPTER 3

A Time *to* Heal

Kendra agonized over her decision to seek a divorce from Marcus. Their marriage had been rocky for several years, with Marcus sliding deeper into substance abuse, despite his repeated promises to confront his problems and change his ways. His attempts were always half-hearted and short-lived. Employment became infrequent and financial troubles common. Worse, Kendra discovered that Marcus had cheated on her.

Kendra tried counseling and even convinced Marcus to go for a few sessions before that ended in failure, with Marcus making endless excuses and telling blatant lies. "If someone can't tell the truth in marriage counseling, there's no point in continuing and very little hope for the relationship," Kendra said.

She knew the marriage was over but didn't want to accept it. Back and forth she went, veering from despondency to hope and back again. When she finally made the decision to start divorce proceedings, she thought things would get better. She thought *she* would get better, but she didn't.

Kendra was unprepared for the emotional roller coaster that came with dissolving a twenty-one-year relationship. What about the kids? Who would get the house and the dog? What would happen with their friendships? It was a nightmare. At some point, Kendra just went numb. She could no longer cry. She had no energy to argue. She walked through each day like a zombie.

For Kendra, her coping became a strategy of apathetic acceptance. If it meant another call to the attorney, she

made it. If it meant another legal document to sign, she signed it. If it meant getting her kids ready to spend the weekend with their father, she packed up their things and waved good-bye from the doorway. Kendra was locked in survival mode. No more tears. No more anguish. She told herself it was the only way to get through—the only way to survive.

Yet Kendra wasn't surviving inside; she was dying. No tears meant no laughter either. No more anguish meant no more joy. People became a burden. Most of her friends were happily married and couldn't understand what she was going through. Besides, they were busy with their own lives, and she had more than enough to do every day. Her home became her sanctuary. She stopped going to church, and she always came straight home after work. Slowly, her world shrank until it was only Kendra and her kids.

Kendra's story exemplifies the difficulties that many people struggle with as they experience loss. Confusion turns into desperation. Irritation turns into anger. Disappointment turns into despair. Once the spiral begins, it can pick up speed and turn into lonely isolation and a joyless life.

It doesn't need to be this way! Whatever loss you've experienced and whatever hardship you're struggling with, tending to your hurting heart will bolster every aspect of whole-person wellness. The following principles will help you regain your footing and move toward healing as you grieve your loss.

1 Pay Attention to Your Emotions

Loss produces pain, and no one wants to feel pain. As a result, many people experiencing grief suppress their feelings, avoiding difficult emotions that are a natural part of loss. The problem is that the pain is still there, affecting what you do and how you handle your life. You may think you're not feeling anger, and yet you're harboring a negative attitude and acting hostile toward those around you. You may think you're not frustrated or hurting, but why do small setbacks seem like such large obstacles? The truth is, your feelings are lurking underneath the numbness and denial, causing pain and creating problems. Bringing your feelings out in the light of day allows you to start seeing them for what they are and how they affect you.

TENDING TO YOUR HURTING HEART WILL BOLSTER EVERY ASPECT OF WHOLE-PERSON WELLNESS.

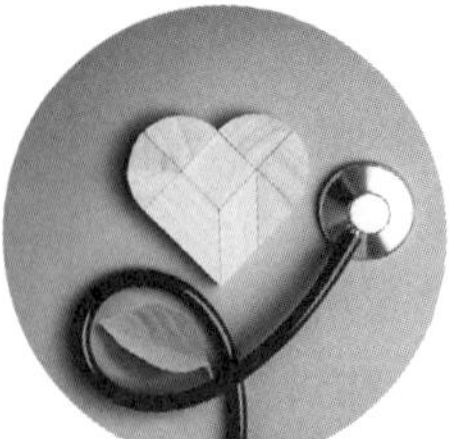

When people have devoted themselves to suppressing their feelings in order to protect themselves from pain, they can become pessimistic and react suspiciously in all situations. They don't remember how to be open to positive emotions and experiences because they've spent so much time closing themselves off. It can be difficult relearning how to cry, enjoy a belly laugh, or tolerate fear, anger, frustration, and pain without becoming emotionally overwhelmed.

Healing means not only recognizing that feelings exist but also allowing them to flow freely. I appreciate the perspective of psychotherapist Julia Samuel, who affirms the need to let grief "rage through us with its full force if we are to process it effectively."[7] Letting grief rage through us can feel intensely painful, so trying to avoid our strong emotions and their powerful impact is understandable. But anyone who has been through grief of some kind will know the futility of trying to prevent it. Experiencing your emotions and processing them in a healthy way is the only way to heal from painful loss.

2 Pay Attention to Your Thoughts

Over the course of four decades, I have counseled thousands of people struggling with every imaginable problem: depression, anxiety, insomnia, eating disorders, addictions, marital failure, and on and on. Every one of these painful situations has confirmed for me a truth I learned years ago in my psychological training: *What goes on in your mind inevitably and irrefutably comes out in your actions, attitudes, and ambitions.*

Your thoughts—the messages you tell yourself every second of every day—profoundly and powerfully determine every other aspect of your life. What you tell yourself *about* yourself can radically influence your happiness, relationships, career, parenting, mental health, and physical well-being. This presents a good news–bad news scenario: If your thoughts are consistently affirming, optimistic, and constructive, your life is sure to advance in a positive direction. But if your thoughts are consistently critical, pessimistic, or destructive, your life will advance in a negative direction.

I am sure you like the sound of a *positive* rather than *negative* direction. So begin paying close attention to your self-talk—all those silent but powerful internal messages you continually send yourself. Nurture the helpful, healing thoughts while banishing the ones that bring you down and cause you doubt. As my colleague Les Parrott explains,

> Most of the time we have little conscious awareness of our own internal dialogue. And yet this "self-talk" has a huge impact on how you feel about yourself. It is the single most important determiner of whether or not you feel profound significance at your core. Your self-talk is a primary tool for realizing your lovability.... Healthy persons are keenly aware of what they say to themselves, how they say it, and when they say it.[8]

For all of us, that inner voice aggressively seeks to remind us of not only our losses but also our faults, failures, and other unfortunate experiences. Yet it is within your power to control the on-off switch for that voice and to choose which ideas you feed and which you starve. Old ways of thinking often put up a fierce fight when challenged by something new, but you are not a mere bystander witnessing a boxing match between good thoughts and bad thoughts.

Refuse to think too long about past hurts and redirect your thoughts to uplifting memories. Reject self-inflicted verbal beatings and replace them with positive affirmations. Accept your shortcomings and celebrate your strengths. What a difference it would make if your self-talk were affirmative and hopeful, with messages like these:

- *This unexpected layoff has been truly painful, but I choose to trust that it will lead to an even better employment situation for me.*

ACCEPT YOUR SHORTCOMINGS AND CELEBRATE YOUR STRENGTHS.

- *It's hard to believe that we'll never celebrate Mom's birthday again, but when that day rolls around this year, I'll try to remember the fun and meaningful celebrations we had in the past.*
- *I'm still feeling disoriented after my confidence was betrayed, but I believe I will be able to work through the shock and become even stronger.*
- *It was hard visiting the site where our house once stood before the hurricane. My emotions have been on a roller coaster ride, but at least my ups and downs are becoming less frequent.*

When you use self-talk like this, a new pathway of healing strength will open up, carrying you another step closer to your goal of achieving wellness in every area of your life. Your subconscious hears all and believes all, so feed it positive, constructive thoughts as you cling to hope.

3 Talk It Through

When we share our thoughts and feelings with someone who's willing to listen, many benefits follow. First, it helps us verbalize what's inside. This itself can shine a light on the path forward, when we actually hear our internal thoughts expressed externally. Second, talking with someone is an active step toward a solution, even if the solution isn't immediately evident. Third, talking gives us a chance to hear the helpful perspectives of others. I agree with psychologist Georgia Witkin, who describes talking as "one of our natural, built-in, therapeutic capacities. We use our words to express what we want and need, and the same should be for our feelings."[9]

Whether it's talking with a counselor, clergyman, or trusted friend, expressing your thoughts and feelings in words will foster healing. But as you might suspect, I am a big believer in engaging in therapy with a skilled, experienced practitioner. A sign of emotional health is the willingness to access professional resources in times of need. Sometimes problems are so pressing that outside assistance is vital, and taking advantage of it demonstrates wisdom and courage.

As you continue the journey toward stability, it's crucial that you continue getting regular professional help through counseling, for as long as necessary. Grief can be an especially deep-rooted issue, and many people benefit tremendously from the guidance and insights of a qualified therapist or counselor who can provide a place of safety to explore painful emotions and tailor a plan to pursue wellness. Seeking professional guidance is especially important if you find that your experience of loss is plunging you into depression or even suicidal thoughts.

One form of talk therapy is called Dialectical Behavior Therapy (DBT), which is a clear and effective process for working through strong emotions and shifting them

from harmful to helpful. Using this technique or others, a compassionate practitioner can show you how emotions stemming from loss have turned into maladapted behaviors—and equip you to exchange negative responses for constructive ones. With God's help and a counselor's encouragement, you can move forward on a healthy path. Another idea is to seek out a grief support group in your area, which provides a safe, welcoming place for people to process the difficult emotions of grief with others who have experienced a loss.

GRIEFSHARE

GriefShare is a well-established grief support program that facilitates in-person and online support groups in thousands of locations throughout the US and around the world. Groups are led by a trained facilitator and last thirteen weeks. Each gathering begins with a half-hour video presentation by a mental health expert, followed by group discussion on the topic covered. The organization's website says that "since there are no neat, orderly stages of grief, you'll learn helpful ways of coping with grief, in all its unpredictability—and gain solid support each step of the way." You can learn more at GriefShare.org.

4 Journal Your Thoughts and Feelings

The value of processing your loss by talking with others cannot be overstated, but additional benefits are gained when you take time to write out your thoughts and feelings. Journaling your story has great power, since each time you chronicle a struggle, you contribute to your handbook of how to overcome loss both now and in the future. In essence, you are writing your own self-help book.

Expressive writing of your thoughts and feelings can help lessen anxiety and depression. James Pennebaker and John Evans, authors of the book *Expressive Writing: Words That Heal,* state that "across multiple studies, people who engage in expressive writing report feeling happier and less negative than they felt before writing. Similarly, reports of depressive symptoms, rumination, and general anxiety tend to drop in the weeks and months after writing about emotional upheavals."[10]

CHOOSE A TIME TO WRITE AND REFLECT ON YOUR GRIEF JOURNEY.

Pennebaker and Evans also explain that using words such as *because, realize,* and *understand* highlights the relationship between cause and effect. It helps you to place your difficult loss in the context of your larger life story, as well as to acknowledge the personal growth that resulted. As your brain begins to make sense of your experience in this way, your painful emotions are soothed.

You don't need to write down everything in the moment, but you can choose a time—perhaps when things calm down—to write and reflect on your grief journey. Put aside any anxiety about writing polished prose or poetic imagery. Don't fret that others will read what you've written—or that what you write will not be good enough. Once you start the habit of writing out your thoughts and emotions, you'll be surprised at the effect of this simple tool for processing your loss.

5 Live in the Present

Feelings associated with grief often negatively shift our perspective on the past, present, and future. Do you sometimes find yourself wondering, *What if . . . ?* There are an infinite number of ways to complete that sentence. Depending on our circumstances and our choices, life is full of potentially different outcomes. *What ifs* can inspire us to hope, fill us with regret, or haunt us with fear of poverty, lack, and abandonment. When dealing with loss, our *What ifs* are mostly negative:

- *What if I had been more careful to check out the reviews for this business? I could have saved myself from being scammed.*
- *What if I'm not able to get over my heartbreak? I can't imagine staying stuck in this pit of depression and hopelessness.*
- *What if I get laid off and can't pay the mortgage? What if our car breaks down and we can't afford to repair or replace it?*

Against this relentless tide, we relive the pain of past losses or worry about difficulties that could lie ahead. We build fragile levies out of anything we can stockpile—for example, money, possessions, or job status. *Surplus* and *security* have come to mean the same thing, but the truth is, the whole world doesn't contain enough material wealth to cover all possible *What ifs*. In addition to financial uncertainties, there are plenty of other potential personal and relational losses that are beyond our control to know about or prevent.

Therefore, it is helpful to stop and go back to the basics of affirming the promise and potential of *this* day—not fretting about past losses or worrying about what tomorrow may bring. A good way to incorporate this practice is by reading or reciting the Lord's Prayer—a prayer that Jesus taught his disciples—with a focus on this sentence: "Give us today our daily bread" (Matthew 6:11). Notice two key words: *today* and *daily*. They point out that all we really need is provision for this moment in time.

Praying for "daily bread"—for just enough provision to live this day—isn't something we would come up with on our own. I'm pretty sure that if human beings had written this portion of the Lord's Prayer, it would have gone something like this:

- "Give us this day … the full amount needed for our monthly expenses."
- "Give us this day … the assurance that we will never lose a loved one before they reach old age."
- "Give us this day … wisdom to navigate the next painful loss that will inevitably come our way."

You might have heard the old saying, "Enough is as good as a feast." But the truth is that few of us really believe it. Today's feast never quite satisfies our hunger to know whether there will be enough financial or emotional currency for tomorrow, especially after experiencing the consequences of a heartbreaking loss.

"GIVE US TODAY OUR DAILY BREAD."
—Matthew 6:11

Fortunately, God has an alternate plan. Unlike earthly strategies, his way is immune to every misfortune and disaster. He offers us the only true source of security—a relationship with himself. Don't misunderstand: God doesn't wave a magic wand and make uncertainty disappear. Instead, every new and frightening *What if* has a single solution: faith in God's promise to care for us—today. It isn't necessary to know where his provision is stored or how it will reach us tomorrow. The secret to real security lies in choosing to take Jesus at his Word:

> Don't worry about these things, saying, "What will we eat? What will we drink? What will we wear?" These things dominate the thoughts of unbelievers, but your heavenly Father already knows all your needs. Seek the Kingdom of God above all else, and live righteously, and he will give you everything you need. So don't worry about tomorrow, for tomorrow will bring its own worries. Today's trouble is enough for today.
>
> MATTHEW 6:31–34 NLT

When Jesus taught us to pray for daily bread, he was reminding us to put our trust in God alone. That's an investment that always pays a dividend—and helps keep our losses in proper perspective. After all, what could be more secure than living by faith each day in the care of the living God?

6 Express Yourself Creatively

Human beings have practiced creative expression for thousands of years, fostering mental and emotional health and well-being. In addition to journaling and expressive writing, art forms such as music, drama, dance, sculpture, and other means of self-exploration and self-expression can be equally therapeutic.

One study reported that regardless of a person's artistic ability, forty-five minutes of creative activity lessened their stress and improved their mental health.[11] Additionally, according to Resources to Recover,

- "Studies suggest that art therapy can be very valuable in treating issues such as depression, anxiety, post-traumatic stress disorder and even some phobias. It is a great way to express your emotions without words, process complex feelings, and find relief."
- Research shows that "creating art stimulates the release of dopamine. This chemical is released when we do something pleasurable, and it basically makes us feel happier. Increased levels

of this feel-good neurotransmitter can be very helpful if you are battling anxiety or depression."[12]

Consider pursuing a variety of creative expressions to significantly reduce the hardship and heartache related to loss. When practiced regularly, these outlets help you process loss in ways that facilitate healing as you explore your emotions, increase self-awareness, bolster self-esteem, and find new ways to deal with stress.

7 Surround Yourself with Life-Giving People

It matters tremendously who we surround ourselves with, especially when faced with the inevitable ups and downs that accompany grieving a loss. We can't always select the people who fill our lives, but we *can* choose the people we want to be close to.

Have you ever felt that you were letting people you encountered throughout the day determine your mood? If they were angry about something, you adopted the same stance. If they were pleasant and cordial, you jumped on the same happy wagon. If they were grumpy, you found yourself becoming irritable.

Psychologists call this phenomenon "emotional contagion" or "mood transference," which means that one person's emotions can directly trigger similar emotions in others. If these brief episodes can influence us so strongly, just imagine the long-term effects generated by people we spend time with on a regular basis. Each of those interactions accumulates over time to shape us into who we are.

Think for a moment about the people whose company you value and cherish. Recall those who make a difference in your life for the positive. They are interested in you and invested in you. They share their life with you and encourage you to do the same. They pick you up when you fall down. The most fulfilling marriages, dating relationships, and friendships involve people who genuinely want each other to experience a life of happiness, meaning, and fulfillment. They offer continual encouragement and look for practical ways to help one another excel. Such collective strength contributes to the blessings of a mutually supportive relationship.

When we find an ally who will challenge us to go after something better, support us in the attempt, and cheer us on in its achievement, we must strive to keep that friendship alive and well. We all need to surround ourselves with people who, without being judgmental, will accept us for who we are and yet call us to a bigger, bolder life by helping us move out of our comfort zone and take giant steps forward toward our goals.

8 Guard Against Joy-Stealers

Just as we should be intentional about inviting supportive friends into our lives, we need to be equally intentional about guarding against people who bring us down. Having healthy relational boundaries will keep toxic people from undermining the healing we seek. The less we allow an invasion of the joy-stealers, the less poison we will take into our own system.

I'd like you to put up a mental "boundary crossing" sign to help remind you how others may have overstepped their privileges in the past—and may even continue to do so in the present. Maybe you have someone in your life who makes you feel inadequate and unworthy of seeking the healing you need to reach your full potential. Perhaps you have well-meaning but negative friend or family influences. Summon the courage to hold firm boundaries with manipulative or mean-spirited people—because rebounding from hardship and heartache depends on it.

9 Accept Support from Others

In the wake of loss, people who are hurting often are unwilling to ask for or accept practical support and help when it's offered. This might be because they don't want to be "a bother" or they don't want others to feel sorry for them—or they wrongly believe that seeking help is a sign of weakness.

To Ruth, having other people in her life meant she was responsible to give to them. That's how she was raised, so she put it into practice by giving to her husband until he died. She'd given to her kids until they moved away. She had cared for friends and neighbors in times of need.

SUMMON THE COURAGE TO HOLD FIRM BOUNDARIES.

But when Ruth became mired in severe depression after the loss of her closest friend, she chose to muddle through on her own instead of reaching out to her daughter and son. When friends asked how she was doing, she said "Fine" and quickly changed the subject. If they offered to bring her a meal or clean her house, Ruth's immediate reaction was, "Thanks, but that's not necessary." Her job was to give to others, not accept charity. But the deeper her depression, the less Ruth had to give and the more she withdrew from others.

The best and healthiest relationships are reciprocal, with both people giving and taking as the occasion warrants. None of us are immune to the challenges of life, and when they arise, we need to draw upon the strength of others to persevere. Ruth pushed away people who would have been blessed by offering her a helping hand.

As you struggle to heal from grief, don't be afraid to ask for help. Don't be so prideful that you're ashamed of your needs. Don't allow fatigue or exhaustion to derail your relationships. Allow others to build you up and to help in practical ways. There will come a time when you have the blessing of comforting and assisting others again because of what you've gained through this experience.

10 Bring Joy Back into Your Journey

It's probably safe to say that one thing you've forgotten through your struggle with loss and grief is how to have *fun*. But if you're disheartened enough, you may just roll your eyes and mumble that "fun" is for other people. You might think that enjoyment in daily life happens only for others. I know, because that's how I felt after months of having all my senses—including my sense of humor—bleached and hung out to dry during a time of difficulty.

But it's instructive to notice that *enjoyment* refers to the process of taking pleasure in something. *Process. Taking.* These are active words, things we purposely do and participate in. You can sit and wait for joy to strike spontaneously, and it sometimes does. But why would you want to wait when it's possible to make it happen for yourself? As with so many other things we've discussed, the power of enjoyment—even after suffering loss—is triggered by choice.

Start by silencing your inner critic, who pronounces judgment on every possible source of fun before you even try it. *A rafting excursion?* Too wet, too dangerous. *A salsa dance class with friends?* Too embarrassing. *A day at the amusement park?* Too childish, too expensive, too loud, too many lines.

The good news is, it's possible to displace objections like these with a determined decision to "just do it." Will this test the boundaries of your comfort zone? Of course, but that's one aspect of what makes it fun.

11 Cuddle Your Pet (or Adopt One)

It may not surprise you to know that having a pet offers many benefits beyond mere companionship. In one pet-owner survey, nearly eight out of ten participants reported experiencing improved personal health as a result of owning a pet, and nearly nine out of ten reported improvements in their mental health.[13] In another study, employees who brought their dogs to work scored significantly higher in job satisfaction and showed a decline in stress throughout the day, while their canine-free coworkers reported an increase.[14]

But why, exactly, do pets have a therapeutic influence on our mental and physical health? According to researchers who analyzed sixty-nine studies on human-animal interactions, an increase in the production of the hormone oxytocin might account for the reduced stress and improved mood experienced by many pet owners.[15]

Beyond scientific explanation, animal friends provide their owners with the pleasure of cuddling, company, and—in the case of dogs who need to be walked—exercise and sunlight. Cheryl Christopher sums up these sentiments well in her book *A Portrait of Grief*:

> There is a reason therapy dogs are allowed in hospitals, nursing homes, and airplanes. They bring comfort. They improve blood pressure and enhance brain chemistry. With loving eyes and wagging tails, they assure us that everything will be okay.[16]

In addition, pets make us smile. They give us reason to laugh. They change the subject of each day from sorrow to happiness, the narrative of our journey from devastating loss to new life. They give us needed love at a time when it matters most.

12 Beware of Roadblocks

As you take the preceding steps to heart, watch out for behaviors and choices that will do nothing but keep you stuck in place. Here are a few examples.

Denial

Denial is one of the five stages of grief that we discussed in the previous chapter. Because the emotions that accompany grief are painful, we tend to avoid them. But in order to heal, sorrow and loss must eventually be acknowledged and accepted. One of the more persistent barriers to healing is the false idea that moving beyond a tragic loss in your life diminishes that loss. Resist the concept that the only way to be true to your loss is to keep the wound fresh. You are free to move forward trusting that God will bring redemption.

Isolation

Living through a crisis can feel like you're trudging through each day, and interacting with other people seems to take too much energy. Yet study after study shows that supportive relationships are essential to improving how we experience and process grief. In fact, loneliness is linked to not only depression but also health problems such as high blood pressure, cardiovascular disease, cancer, and cognitive decline. Other studies show that people who are involved in faith communities tend to have lower levels of anxiety and stress.

False Guilt

Have you ever experienced a sense of guilt about something, even though you had done nothing wrong? Grieving people sometimes blame themselves for somehow contributing to a loss, even if they were not at fault. It colors the way they look at themselves. False guilt preys on people who have an overly sensitive conscience. It tricks them into questioning their motives and mentally chastising themselves for something they didn't do.

SUPPORTIVE RELATIONSHIPS ARE ESSENTIAL FOR PROCESSING GRIEF.

On the other hand, healthy guilt that occurs after we've truly erred helps us ask forgiveness from those we've hurt, repair what might be broken, set boundaries, and plot a better course for the future. How do you tell the difference between false guilt and healthy guilt? One way is simply to ask yourself, *Is there a legitimate reason that I'm feeling guilty about this situation, or am I believing lies?* Be truly honest with yourself, and the answer should reveal itself.

Negative Escapes and "Painkillers"

When we experience grief, it's tempting to turn to behaviors such as excessive eating or spending or substance abuse. Of course, that's because we want to do something to change our mood! The list of unhelpful and unhealthy escapes could go on and on. Numbing your pain can alter how you feel about your loss and may briefly help you function through the worst of your pain, but it will never change your circumstances or remove your loss. Self-medicating does not—and cannot—make anything go away.

Neglecting Healthy Habits

To make matters worse, it's also tempting to let healthy lifestyle practices go by the wayside when we are consumed by trying to cope with our heartache. We reach for comfort food, stop exercising, and allow disruptions to our sleep routine. Doing so hinders the healing process, since one of the best ways to foster recovery is to fortify our bodies. Eating right, getting enough sleep, and exercising regularly are habits that relieve feelings of stress and anxiety, improve our mood, and energize our bodies.

Just as there is no preset method or timetable for grieving your loss, you will not find a one-size-fits-all template for healing after loss. One thing is certain, however: Healing is most effective when you intentionally choose the principles introduced in this chapter—without holding yourself to rigid expectations that you will follow them perfectly. As you practice them with consistency and dedication, you will see progress. Along the way, you have the opportunity to embrace another potent source of healing that brings life to all your efforts. Read on to find out more.

STEPPING STONES TO HEALING

1. **Journal your thoughts and feelings.** As you think about your loss, write down the struggles you have faced and the feelings you have encountered. Don't hold back in expressing your deepest emotions. Being honest with yourself is a mark of integrity.

   Takeaways: ______________________________

   ____

   ____

   ____

   ____

2. **Reframe distorted thoughts.** Write down a negative or self-critical thought that is hindering you; then reframe it to make a positive statement. For instance, change *I'll never get over this* to *I have the inner strength and support of others to work through this.*

   Negative thought: ______________________________

   ____

   ____

   Reframed thought: ______________________________

   ____

   ____

3. **Make plans for artistic enjoyment.** Do you favor a particular form of artistic expression? There are so many options—dance, music, painting, ceramics, acting, creative writing ... the list is endless! Even if you don't feel gifted in one of these areas, enjoying the artistic works of others can also be therapeutic.

   My plan: ______________________________

4. **Have fun!** Plan a dinner out with friends, enjoy a nature hike, go on a minivacation, or do whatever else brings you delight. Don't let anything stand in the way of bringing joy back into your journey.

   My plan: ______________________________

CHAPTER 4

Prioritize Spiritual Care

Unlike many who are weighed down by grief, Eva's descent had not been triggered by a single traumatic event. After a series of draining and disappointing losses, she let the devastating effects compound instead of dealing with them as they came along. This led to her slow spiral from disappointment to discouragement to depression.

At this point in her life, Eva found herself stuck in a mediocre job with little promise of advancement. Her romantic prospects were minimal, as she rarely had more than one or two dates with the same person. And although she tried to put some money into savings each month, it seemed that unexpected expenses would always gobble up whatever funds she had managed to save.

On top of such disheartening circumstances, Eva had also been gaining weight and feeling tired. She wasn't suffering from any specific kind of illness, but she often woke up weary and reluctant to face the morning. Her energy and outlook usually dwindled by midafternoon, and on most evenings and weekends she felt numb. What little solace she had found came from less-than-healthy comfort foods, consumed as she slouched on her sofa, streaming one show after another.

At the urging of a friend, Eva entered therapy with a skilled counselor who helped her talk through many emotional difficulties that stemmed from her losses. Eva's counselor also coached her in adopting healthier nutrition, exercise, sleep, and thought-life habits. All of this helped improve her circumstances and her outlook, yet Eva still felt like something was missing.

Then one day Eva had coffee with Leticia, a friend who had recently moved back to the area. Leticia was typically upbeat, with a sparkle in her eyes that helped lift the spirits of everyone around her. As Eva updated Leticia on her string of losses and the sense that she was lacking something important in her healing journey, Leticia listened closely and asked questions to make sure she understood what Eva was going through.

Their coffee time turned out to be a breakthrough for Eva. As they talked, Leticia was able to perceive what was missing from Eva's campaign against depression, and she suggested an idea that would enlist the greatest power in the universe to help stabilize Eva's emotional life.

"You have taken so many positive and intentional steps forward," Leticia told her, "and now it's time to realize the importance of your spiritual life. Without leaning into God's power and his gracious offer of friendship in our lives, our other efforts will fall short of their full potential to bring healing into our lives."

Eva thought about this for a moment, then nodded her head in agreement. "I think you're right. I've been diligent about establishing lots of healthy habits to pull myself out of depression, but my spiritual life has been as dry as a desert."

"All right, then," Leticia said, "let's work together to sprinkle water on that dry ground. I'm all in. I would love to meet with you once a week for the next three months to read Scripture and pray together if you're up for it."

Eva enthusiastically accepted Leticia's gracious invitation, and the process of reengaging Eva's spiritual life began. Revitalizing her relationship with God was a big step forward in healing her depression. It was a choice she had to make, with the help of an invested friend. Perhaps you, too, have a friend who can walk with you on that journey. But even if you don't, there are many ways you can take the initiative to strengthen your spiritual journey. Let's take a look at five of them.

1 Choose Faith

So often in times of crisis, when well-meaning people advise you to "have faith," they often make it sound simple, as if it's possible to magically "have" something as elusive as faith on command. That's nearly as unhelpful as telling someone who's suffering from depression to simply "feel better."

In previous chapters, you've learned that every step on the path to healing requires courage and commitment on your part—all summed up in one powerful word: *choice*. You must choose to seek help and choose to pursue the remedies you are offered, before you can tap in to their healing potential.

Faith is no different. It's not an ethereal "thing" we try to grasp. Having faith requires action. It's something we do on purpose. True, God is willing and able to meet you exactly where you are and to carry you for as long as it takes to restore your strength. But faith is our part to play in order to actively complete the circuit of God's love. We do that by choosing to believe we are not alone—through sheer force of will, if necessary—even when the night is at its darkest.

Because faith begins with a determined choice, it is a jolt of energy that activates your spiritual and emotional immune system like nothing else can. How? By opening the door to the one thing you may feel you've lost forever: *hope*. As the writer of the book of Hebrews assures us, "Faith is confidence in what we hope for and assurance about what we do not see" (11:1). That writer knew what it meant to hope for something we can't yet see—and understood that active, determined faith bridges the gap while we wait for and work toward whatever it is that we are trusting will materialize.

Having faith means you can *know* you'll eventually receive what you seek, because your faith doesn't rest in fate or chance. Your faith is in God, who is unfailingly good. One way or another, you always choose how to face your life—with confidence or with doubt, in strength or in defeat. Given those options, why not choose the power of faith?

2 Talk Daily with God

Prayer can be considered an ongoing dialogue with God, a continual conversation with him. Heartfelt and honest conversation with God is yours for the having. Since God is all-knowing and all-seeing, he is aware of everything about your life whether you talk to him or not. But he loves you so much that he is eager to spend time with you beyond simply listening to a list of requests that you bring to him. Amid the struggles of your loss, you can ask for wisdom and guidance as you share your feelings and fears and talk about your everyday concerns. Everyone on earth could use divine direction and understanding in their daily lives—and this is especially true for those who are dealing with grief. Prayer is a powerful source of insight and inspiration as you rebound from

> "FAITH IS CONFIDENCE IN WHAT WE HOPE FOR AND ASSURANCE ABOUT WHAT WE DO NOT SEE."
>
> –Hebrews 11:1

hardship and heartache. Consider talking with God about these topics:

- Possessing the strength to face the future with courage
- Maintaining gratitude for the good things in your life and the ways you have grown stronger through your loss
- Pursuing opportunities to overcome your loss by utilizing the talents and passions God has given you
- Having wisdom to consistently make choices that show respect for yourself and others
- Guiding you steadily toward strength and comfort in your body, mind, soul, and spirit

3 Listen Closely to God's Voice

The book of Ecclesiastes states there is not only "a time to mourn" (3:4) and "a time to heal" (3:3), but also "a time to be silent" (3:7). After all, prayer is a *conversation*—two-way communication. Some people scoff at the idea that God speaks back, but only because they've never heard an audible voice answer them directly. The truth is, God speaks all the time, and we would have no trouble hearing him if we'd only broaden our definition of speech. Psalm 19:1–4 says,

> The heavens declare the glory of God; the skies proclaim the work of his hands.... They have no speech, they use no words; no sound is heard from them. Yet their voice goes out into all the earth, their words to the ends of the world.

As this psalm so eloquently describes, God certainly speaks through nature. That message is one of majesty and grandeur to be sure, but also of balance, beauty, and rebirth—qualities we can cling to when grieving a loss.

But that's just the beginning. Go looking for the diverse love notes from God that fill the world, and you will find them. His voice can be heard in art and music, in stories that inspire us to be more and do better. He speaks in every act of kindness, no matter how small. God's part of the conversation is found in the Scriptures and in the words of wise people throughout time who've labored to bring light into the darkness of ignorance. God speaks in our dreams and in subtle moments of intuition.

PRAYER IS A *CONVERSATION*— TWO-WAY COMMUNICATION.

But, like in every conversation, it's possible to not hear a word of it. Until you choose to believe that God will actually answer your questions and calm your fears, it's likely you'll frantically do all the talking and never make room for his reply. Read on to discover tips for avoiding this unnecessary mistake by slowing down, setting aside time to be quiet, and extending your awareness.

4 Seek Moments of Stillness

Often when we are trying to rebound from the heartache of loss and grief, the hardest thing to do is to follow God's instructions in Psalm 46:10: "Be still, and know that I am God." But to process painful emotions, we need to slow down so we can encounter the healing presence of God. And in order to truly slow down and quiet our inner self, a few things need to occur:

1. We need to retreat from the distractions of the world.
2. We must make a conscious effort to calm our minds.
3. We need to face our present realities—both internally and externally.

This three-step process is difficult; it takes energy and commitment, and it means being fully honest with yourself and with God and facing the pain of any discomforting or negative emotions and thoughts. It means turning off the noises and clutter in our brains and listening to what God may be saying to us.

There are a myriad of ways to get quiet and allow God to speak to you. One of the simplest ways is to go somewhere safe and quiet where you feel relaxed. If, when you try to quiet your mind, you are inundated with tasks on your mental to-do list, keep a pad of paper and a pen next to you and write down those items so they can be dealt with later. Then, once you are truly in a peaceful place, allow God to minister to you. That may sound old-fashioned, but the verb *minister* simply means allowing God to attend to your hurts, negative emotions, and self-doubt.

ONCE YOU ARE IN A PEACEFUL PLACE, ALLOW GOD TO MINISTER TO YOU.

The first time (or first few times) you try this quieting exercise, you may find it difficult. But like any other spiritual discipline, with continued practice you will be able to enter into a deeper sense of God's peace and presence.

5 Find Solace in Serving Others

Once you establish a two-way conversation with God and realize that he is with you on your healing journey, the next step is to reach outside yourself to make a difference in someone else's life. Faith communities usually excel at providing volunteer opportunities and steering you to one that's right for you. But you can also find ample places to serve in other community organizations, such as

- homeless shelters;
- counseling centers for victims of domestic violence;
- animal rescue organizations;
- wounded veterans' programs;
- hospice care;
- cancer support groups;
- suicide prevention clinics; and
- nursing homes filled with people who need a friend.

All these organizations depend on volunteers who know what it's like to grieve a loss. Best of all, the benefit of your service is twofold, bringing healing to yourself as well as those you help. One study even concluded that people who volunteer in service to others actually live longer than those who don't.[17] By volunteering to help serve your community, you essentially write yourself a prescription that will provide some measure of relief from your own troubles—free of charge. Serving others turns your pain into a blessing to those being served. As the revered priest Henri Nouwen taught,

> The main question is not "How can we hide our wounds?" but "How can we put our woundedness in the service of others?" When our wounds cease to be a source of shame and become a source of healing, we have become wounded healers.[18]

■ ■ ■

When loss invades your life, it leaves an unwelcome legacy of emotional distress, relationship strain, physical symptoms, and spiritual confusion. Yet as you allow yourself to grieve, make determined steps toward healing, and prioritize your spiritual care, you are building strong resilience. The pain of loss is great, but your suffering is not without redemption. In the next chapter, we'll explore some of the lessons of loss that can shape your future for the better.

STEPPING STONES TO HEALING

1. **Ask for divine help.** Jesus told his followers, "Everyone who asks receives; the one who seeks finds; and to the one who knocks, the door will be opened" (Matthew 7:8). No prayer is more powerful than a simple plea for help. Ask God for wisdom as you navigate your loss and make decisions that will foster healing.

   My prayer: ______________________________

   ____

   ____

   ____

   ____

   ____

2. **Seek a spiritual mentor.** If you have questions about the value and practice of faith, rest assured you're not the first one to ask them. Others have walked the road ahead of you and can share what they've learned. Inquiring at a local church or ministry is a great way to start your search for a spiritual mentor.

   Places to start my search: ______________________________

   ____

   ____

   ____

3. **Read the Bible.** The Bible is God's very own Word to us and demonstrates the loving, nurturing, healing nature of our Creator and his desire to bring us back to himself in a world marred by sin. A good place to start is the Gospel of John.

   Takeaways: ______________________________

   ____

   ____

   ____

   ____

4. **Look into opportunities to serve others—then do it.** Check for volunteer opportunities by talking with leaders at your place of worship, by asking friends about places you might serve, or by searching online for local opportunities. The next step is to choose an option and follow through with it.

   Opportunities to serve: ____________________

   ____

   ____

   ____

   ____

CHAPTER 5

The Lessons *of* Loss

Chelsea's phone vibrated with an incoming text. She smiled when she read the simple reminder: "Sister dinner tonight!"

For years, despite living in the same city, Chelsea and her two sisters were so busy that they rarely saw each other apart from holidays, family birthdays, weddings, and funerals.

Then her sister Becky came up with the idea of sister dinners. Every three months the women would meet at a favorite restaurant to catch up in ways they simply couldn't while surrounded by a crowd of people at Thanksgiving or Christmas.

That night, Chelsea, Becky, and Katie met at a local Italian restaurant. It was the week after Christmas, and the dining room was still decorated for the holidays.

After rounds of hugs, the women ordered their favorite dishes and enjoyed salad and breadsticks while waiting for their entrées to arrive.

"What a year, right?" Katie said, the first to broach deeper waters. Ten months earlier, she had been laid off from her job and was still trying to find her footing.

"Tell me about it," Chelsea responded, stroking the place on her finger once occupied by her wedding band.

As for Becky, she was dealing with her own pain as a single parent who was grieving the loss of her relationship with her only child—a twenty-year-old daughter who wanted little to do with family. Becky reached across the table, and the three women clasped hands.

Over the course of the evening, the siblings shared from their hearts.

"When I lost my job, I felt rejected and irrelevant," Katie admitted. "Sometimes I dream that my former boss is begging me to come back. I'm not sure why, because starting my own business has been good for me. But that doesn't erase the shame, sadness, and rejection I feel every time I think—or dream—about my former job and colleagues."

When Chelsea talked about her recent divorce, she teared up. "It seems like all the parts of my life were filling a bucket that was suddenly turned over. I'm trying to put everything back in, but so much of my life doesn't belong there anymore. I'm lost and overwhelmed by the empty space in my bucket—and all these broken pieces on the ground."

Becky's pain over her estranged daughter was so palpable that her sisters didn't think she would want to talk about it. When she did, they listened with breaking hearts.

"I feel like I don't have a family," Becky lamented. Then she added quickly, "Of course I have both of you, but I mean a family of my own. I never thought at this stage in my life I'd feel so alone. I don't have much energy for anything. I don't feel like there's much reason to get out of bed in the morning, other than going to work, which thankfully I do still enjoy."

In the following months, the women continued trying to make sense of their losses while rebuilding aspects of their lives. Their quarterly sister dinners were essential for mutual support and sharing.

The following January, roughly a year after meeting at the Italian restaurant, the sisters convened at another favorite eatery. As they were warmed by a few cups of hot chocolate, their conversation flowed from the trivial to the heartbreaking and back again. Each sister had stories to tell of progress and setbacks, moments of pain and moments of healing. It was clear that Becky, Katie, and Chelsea were not the same people they had been a year prior.

Blessings *in* Disguise

As discussed earlier, loss can look very different from person to person. The types of losses we endure—and our responses to them—cover a broad spectrum. But there are two undeniable truths about loss:

1. Everyone experiences loss.
2. Loss always changes us, sometimes in unexpected ways.

Of course, we're not surprised when loss leaves us feeling sad or empty or forces us to navigate unpleasant memories. But if we're willing to pay attention, we often discover that loss also transforms us in ways we are grateful for, even if we wouldn't wish to repeat the painful event ever again. Let's look at four unexpected ways that loss can bring blessings in disguise.

1 Passion for What Matters Most

After several unexplained seizures, Montrell, a tech consultant, was hospitalized and undergoing testing when his wife, Camille, received a breast cancer diagnosis. Talk about having your world rocked! This couple's sudden loss of health and vitality left them reeling. To make matters worse, their inability to work, coupled with mounting medical bills, left them financially devastated.

LOSS CAN BRING BLESSINGS IN DISGUISE.

Eight months later, both Montrell and Camille finally made it to the other side of their health emergencies. While doctors couldn't pinpoint the cause, Montrell's seizures never returned. Camille's breast cancer surgery and treatment proved successful, and her oncologist gave her a positive prognosis. It would be a slow crawl back to financial stability, but they were on their way.

In one sense, life was returning to normal—yet it looked nothing like it had prior to the crisis. Before Montrell and Camille were forced to face their own mortality, their marriage had been on shaky ground. Nearly losing each other fueled their desire to fight not only for their lives but also for their marriage.

Forging new depth in our relationships with people we love is not an uncommon gift that loss bestows on us. Loss often compels us to reexamine our priorities and gain new perspective on what matters most. Loss can also reveal kindred spirits when acquaintances and even near strangers rush to our sides with practical help and encouragement. They become unexpected lifelines and dear friends in the process.

Of course, loss doesn't always draw people closer. Sometimes crises also expose "fake" friends who fall by the wayside. The loss of these relationships can be painful, yet in the end we are no longer hampered by false friends who were never the allies we believed them to be.

2 New Intimacy with Our Creator

Just as our earthly relationships can improve (or worsen) in the wake of loss, intimacy with God can deepen (or drift) as we grieve. But unlike fake friends who drift away when we are in crisis, God never abandons us. His love and compassion toward us don't change when we are in pain.

> "THE LORD IS CLOSE TO THE BROKENHEARTED AND SAVES THOSE WHO ARE CRUSHED IN SPIRIT."
>
> –Psalm 34:18

We can, however, choose to run from him. Perhaps we are inclined to blame him for our loss or blame ourselves and hide our faces in shame. Or maybe we feel too numb to sense his presence, disillusioned over the sharp and painful turn that life has taken.

Yet even in our pain, shame, numbness, and disillusionment, we can make a choice to run to God instead of from him. When we do, we experience the comfort and strength that renewed intimacy with our Creator brings.

Remember Chelsea, one of the three siblings mentioned at the beginning of this chapter? She shared with her sisters that shortly before her divorce was finalized, she wept as she deeply contemplated the pain her children would experience in the wake of their loss. But instead of walking away from her faith or blaming God, Chelsea asked him, through her tears, to draw her children closer to him through this loss. In the following weeks and months, Chelsea not only trusted God with the broken hearts of her children but discovered how to trust him with her own heart as well.

> "BLESSED ARE THOSE WHO MOURN, FOR THEY WILL BE COMFORTED."
>
> –Matthew 5:4

Two years later, Chelsea's oldest daughter, Rosalyn, was invited to share an inspiring message at their church's youth group. Rosalyn asked her mother to come hear her speak, so at the appointed time, Chelsea slipped into a seat in the back of a room filled with several dozen high school kids.

Rosalyn stood at the front and faced the group. "A couple of years ago," she began, "I went through the hardest time of my life. Two weeks after my boyfriend and I broke up, my parents told me they were getting a divorce."

Chelsea closed her eyes. It was true—the divorce had come at an already pain-filled time in Rosalyn's life.

"One night," Rosalyn continued, "I was in the grocery store, shopping for some items my mom asked me to pick up. I was in such emotional pain at the time that I dropped to my knees in the middle of the soda aisle. I dissolved into tears right there on the floor."

Everyone in the room listened silently, waiting for Rosalyn's next words.

"As I sobbed, I felt the presence of God so strongly. He met me right there on that floor, in a way I had never experienced before."

Chelsea could feel her pulse pounding in her ears.

"I know this sounds weird, but in that most horrible season in my life, I was given a gift," Rosalyn said. "To this day, I don't remember how I made it to my car. But I'll never forget the way God comforted me."

After listening to Rosalyn share her story, Chelsea slipped out of the church with tears of gratefulness streaming down her cheeks. God had answered her prayer beyond her wildest dreams. He had used the pain of the divorce to draw her children closer to him.

When we are grieving a deep loss, it's true that we may be tempted to be angry at God for allowing the painful event to take place. But I urge you to run to him anyway, because God understands your feelings. Tell him everything, including the parts you think he won't like. Your emotions, even if they feel ugly and overwhelming to you, won't scare him away. He wants to meet you in your grief.

Meanwhile, Katie, another one of the three siblings mentioned at the beginning of this chapter, was still feeling irrelevant and powerless as she struggled with rejection, panic, and self-doubt. Those are a lot of emotions to work through.

Katie evaluated what she had brought to the table as an employee. Were there gaps in her skills that she could now fill? Were there things she needed to learn about her industry and herself? When Katie took the step of launching her own business, she tried to apply the things she was learning. The journey was surprisingly rewarding.

TELL GOD EVERYTHING, INCLUDING THE PARTS YOU THINK HE WON'T LIKE.

Loss changes us. We've all heard the old adage that hardship can make us bitter or it can make us better. It sounds cliché, but there's truth to be found in that statement. Your loss—as painful as it is—can teach you valuable lessons as you

- learn about your strengths and grow in areas of weakness;

- deepen your empathy and understanding toward others; and
- develop greater resilience, leaving you better equipped to handle future challenges.

4 Unexpected Purpose

We've all read about people who have pursued a particular mission with great passion, impacting untold lives in the process. But when the curtain is drawn back, we sometimes discover that their tireless determination was rooted in personal loss.

For example, in 1988, John Walsh created the television show *America's Most Wanted,* featuring unsolved crime stories that helped put more than 1,400 wanted criminals behind bars. The show ran for over twenty years and helped victimized families find closure. Walsh's passion for justice was fueled by his own personal tragedy: the 1981 kidnapping and murder of his six-year-old son.

Or consider Kristi Thornton, who lost her brother, Caleb, in an alcohol-related car accident. She coped with the pain by sharing her story with high school students across the nation and starting an organization that encourages people to demonstrate acts of kindness.

Kristi says, "You have to make the best out of the worst situations.... This is an opportunity to do nice things for others. You can't change what happened yesterday, but you can help change what happens today."[19]

As for Becky—Chelsea and Katie's sister who was grieving the loss of her relationship with her daughter—she has found comfort and purpose in starting a support group for parents of estranged and troubled children. Close friendships have formed within the group because of their shared pain. Becky calls the group her lifeline and thinks of each relationship as a gift.

■ ■ ■

When we experience loss, it's natural to focus on our pain. Yet when the time is right, we need to take a deep breath and look around to discover that our experience has brought opportunities to grow and learn. These lessons and gifts may not be easy to see at first, but in time their impact will be hard to miss.

STEPPING STONES TO HEALING

1. **Choose to have hope.** Reflect on how you came through past times of loss or difficulty and eventually lived with hope and joy. Take a walk and savor hopeful symbols of life along the way, such as flowers blooming, birds singing, or young children playing.

   Takeaways: ____

   ____

   ____

   ____

   ____

2. **Focus on the positive.** Identify aspects of your life you feel optimistic about–such as work, parenting, marriage, spiritual growth, or creative pursuits–and journal ideas for how you might prioritize and go deeper into these areas.

   Positive areas of my life: ____________________________

   ____

   ____

   ____

   How I can go deeper: ________________________________

   ____

   ____

   ____

3. **Acknowledge how loss has brought growth.** Maybe you have become more sensitive toward others going through hardship. Perhaps you've forged deeper friendships. Adopt an attitude of thanksgiving for how the lessons of loss have made you a more resilient person.

   How I've grown: ________________________________

   ____

   ____

   ____

   ____

4. **Define your purpose.** In what ways, big or small, has loss reshaped your passions and your life's purpose? In what ways can you follow your purpose and help others in the process?

   My purpose: ________________________________

   ____

   ____

   ____

   How I can help others: ________________________

   ____

   ____

   ____

   ____

A CLOSING WORD

Press On *Toward the* Prize

Your life is a story. Like all stories, yours involves a hero (you), a journey (the losses you've experienced and the heartache and hardships you've endured), and a prize (healing and lifelong wellness). In fact, that progression is found in every story ever told, from ancient myths, to fairy tales, to modern blockbuster films.

Embedded in all stories is a blueprint for healing, growth, and development. Struggling with a loss does not represent failure; it's part of being human. Loss is inevitable, but it's also a catalyst for positive change. Joseph Campbell, the great mythologist and author of *Hero with a Thousand Faces*, once wrote, "It is by going down into the abyss that we recover the treasures of life. Where you stumble, there lies your treasure."[20]

But there is another universal truth about heroes you need to know as you look ahead to continuing life's journey. The true heroes found in books, movies, and real-life stories are never content to passively let events happen to them. When things look darkest and all hope seems lost, they refuse to give up or give in. They are tenacious beyond all reason and stubbornly believe in what others say is impossible. They get back up again and again when they're knocked down.

As you press on toward the treasure of healing and wellness after your loss, it's important to dig in your heels and tap into the determination to never, ever let go of your hope. Defend it in the same way that the heroes you admire most would. The apostle Paul wrote, "I focus on this one thing: Forgetting the past and looking forward to what lies ahead, I press on to reach the end of the race and receive the heavenly prize for which God, through Christ Jesus, is calling us" (Philippians 3:13–14 NLT).

As you take note of big and little blessings along the way, your anguish will begin to ease. Your pain will slowly be edged out by peace. And while there will always be sad moments, they will no longer hold power over you as you find your way back to wholeness. With your persistence and God's help, the loss you've experienced will be redeemed for a brighter future.

Notes

1 "Building Your Resilience," last updated February 1, 2020, *American Psychological Association: https://www.apa.org/topics/resilience/building-your-resilience.*

2 "Luckiest Man," accessed June 30, 2025, *National Baseball Hall of Fame: https://baseballhall.org/discover-more/stories/baseball-history/lou-gehrig-luckiest-man.*

3 Debbie Koenig and Neha Pathak, "The Grief Experience: Survey Shows It's Complicated," July 11, 2019, *WebMD: https://www.webmd.com/special-reports/grief-stages/20190711/the-grief-experience-survey-shows-its-complicated.*

4 "Grief," accessed May 20, 2025, *American Psychological Association: https://www.apa.org/topics/grief/.*

5 Mark D. Miller, "Complicated Grief in Late Life," *Dialogues in Clinical Neuroscience* 14, no. 2 (2012):195–202, *https://www.tandfonline.com/doi/full/10.31887/DCNS.2012.14.2/mmiller.*

6 "Dr. Elisabeth Kübler-Ross and The Five Stages of Grief,*" *Elisabeth Kübler-Ross Foundation: https://www.ekrfoundation.org/5-stages-of-grief/5-stages-grief/.*

7 As stated at *The Happiness Lab with Dr. Laurie Santos* (podcast), "The Paradox of Grief," *Pushkin: https://www.pushkin.fm/podcasts/the-happiness-lab-with-dr-laurie-santos/the-paradox-of-grief.*

8 Les Parrott and Neil Clark Warren, *Love the Life You Live* (Tyndale House, 2003), 27, 29.

9 Georgia Witkin, "The Power of Talking: Why Experts Advise to Talk About Your Feelings," August 9, 2018, *Psychology Today: https://www.psychologytoday.com/us/blog/the-chronicles-infertility/201808/the-power-talking.*

10 James W. Pennebaker and John F. Evans, *Expressive Writing: Words That Heal* (Idyll Arbor, 2014), 11.

11 Girija Kaimal, Kendra Ray, and Juan Muniz, "Reduction of Cortisol Levels and Participants' Responses Following Art Making," *Journal of the American Art Therapy Association* 33, no. 2 (May 23, 2016): 74–80, *https://pmc.ncbi.nlm.nih.gov/articles/PMC5004743/.*

12 Mary Ann Cohen, "Creativity and Recovery: The Mental Health Benefits of Art Therapy," July 10, 2018, *https://www.rtor.org/2018/07/10/benefits-of-art-therapy/.*

13 "Habri Benchmark Survey of U.S. Pet Owners," 2021 Survey, *Habri: https://habri.org/2016-pet-owners-survey.*

14 Randolph T. Barker, et al., "Preliminary Investigation of Employee's Dog Presence on Stress and Organizational

Perceptions," *International Journal of Workplace Health Management* 5, no. 1 (March 23, 2012): 15–30, *https://doi.org/10.1108/17538351211215366.*

15 Andrea Beetz et al., "Psychosocial and Psychophysiological Effects of Human-Animal Interactions: The Possible Role of Oxytocin," *Frontiers in Psychology* 3 (July 8, 2012), *https://doi.org/10.3389/fpsyg.2012.00234.*

16 Cheryl Christopher, *A Portrait of Grief* (Trilogy Christian Publishers, 2022), 119.

17 Stephanie L. Brown et al., "Providing Social Support May Be More Beneficial than Receiving It: Results from a Prospective Study of Mortality," *Psychological Science* 14, no. 4 (July 2003): 320–27, *https://doi.org/10.1111/1467-9280.14461.*

18 The Henri Nouwen Society, as quoted at SusieMiller.com, "The Wounded Healer by Henri Nouwen," *https://www.susiemiller.com/the-wounded-healer-by-henri-nouwen/.*

19 Melanie Feuk, "Kindness Campaign, Scholarship Launched After Tragic Death of Kingwood Resident," May 17, 2018, *Kingwood Observer: https://www.chron.com/neighborhood/kingwood/news/article/Kindness-campaign-scholarship-launched-after-12922041.php.*

20 Diane K. Osbon, ed., *Reflections on the Art of Living: A Joseph Campbell Companion* (HarperPerennial, 1995), 24.

MORE RESOURCES FROM DR. GREGORY L. JANTZ

Unmasking Emotional Abuse

Six Steps to Reduce Stress

Ten Tips for Parenting the Smartphone Generation

Five Keys to Dealing with Depression

Seven Answers for Anxiety

Five Keys to Raising Boys

Freedom from Shame

Five Keys to Health and Healing

When a Loved One Is Addicted

40 Answers for Teens' Top Questions

Social Media and Depression

Rebuilding Trust After Betrayal

How to Deal with Toxic People

The Power of Connection

Why Failure Is Never Final

Find Your Purpose in Life

Here Today, Ghosted Tomorrow

Beyond Burnout

Make Peace with Your Past

Healing After Loss